Francis Bacon
Childhood Adventures

Written by
Sara Lee Langsam

Illustrated by
Christine Leonard

AMERISSIS PRESS

Langsam, Sara Lee
Francis Bacon: Childhood Adventures
Amerissis Press, 2021
email: langsalight@gmail.com

Trade paperback: 978-0-578-93320-7

1. Francis Bacon 2. Children's Stories 3. Integrity 4. Good Values 5. Enlightenment

Text copyright © 2021 by Sara Lee Langsam
Amerissis Press

Illustrations copyright ©2021 by Christine Leonard

All rights reserved. No part of this book may be used or reproduced by any means, graphic, electronic, or mechanical, including photocopying, recording, taping, or by any information storage retrieval system without the written permission of the author except in the case of brief quotations in an article or book review.

Printed in the United States of America

Contents

BOOK ONE:
Francis Bacon:
England's True Prince
p. 1

BOOK TWO:
Francis and Anthony:
Inseparable Brothers
p. 35

Francis Bacon
England's True Prince

by Sara Lee Langsam

Illustrated by Christine Leonard

Once upon a time in England there lived a Queen who was beautiful and wise.
She had a baby boy.

Her very good friend Lady Ann Bacon, as was common in those times, helped the Queen raise her baby boy.

Lady Ann also loved the baby very much and raised him as if he were her own son. She called him Francis.

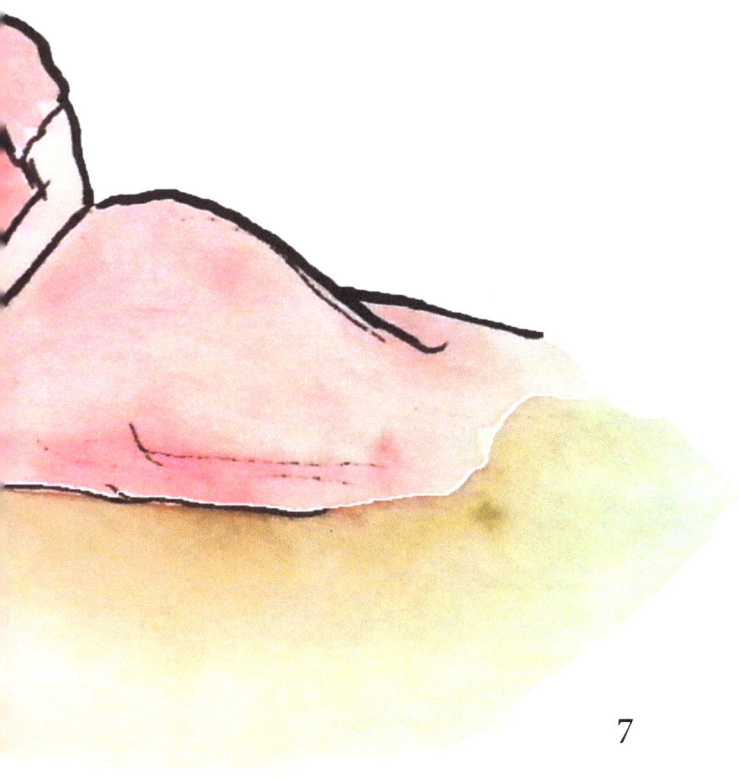

Lady Ann had a son Anthony, who was about two years older than Francis, and the two boys became inseparable.

Francis grew into a boy who was handsome, charming, and lovable.

He was also very intelligent.

He was surrounded by a loving family, and he was very happy.

When Francis was twelve years old, he and Anthony went off to college. They went to study at Trinity College. In those days, children went to college at a very young age.

Francis was a curious boy and wanted to know everything. He wanted to know all there was to know in the whole wide world, and he wanted to share his knowledge with everyone. He had a big heart, and he was a true prince.

Francis had a cousin about his age whose name was Robert. He was also very intelligent.

He did not like Francis and was jealous of him.

One day, he said something unkind to Francis, and Francis hit him. This made Robert very unhappy.

Robert said unkind things about Francis to the Queen. They were not true, but the Queen believed Robert. For this reason, the Queen would not recognize Francis as the Prince that he was.

He had to find another way to help his country.

Francis was ingenious. That means he had great skill in creating and figuring out ways to solve problems. He figured out many different ways to help his country.

He studied to be a lawyer.

He tried to give the Queen good advice.

He wrote books and he wrote plays.

Everyone who saw his plays loved them. They were very funny and made people laugh.

Francis could not admit that he was the author of the plays. In those days it was not considered acceptable for a person like Francis to be a playwright. A playwright is a writer of plays.

Francis had to make believe another person wrote the plays.

No one knew who the real author of the plays was, except a few of Francis' close friends.

Even the Queen did not know, although she enjoyed the plays very much and laughed a lot while watching them.

Today many people know that Francis wrote the plays, but many people still do not know.

In his plays, Francis created many new words that had not been part of the English language.

Francis helped his country and all countries where English was spoken.

He helped many people to understand and experience life in a better way because of the richness of the English language.

We owe a huge debt of gratitude to Francis Bacon.

The End

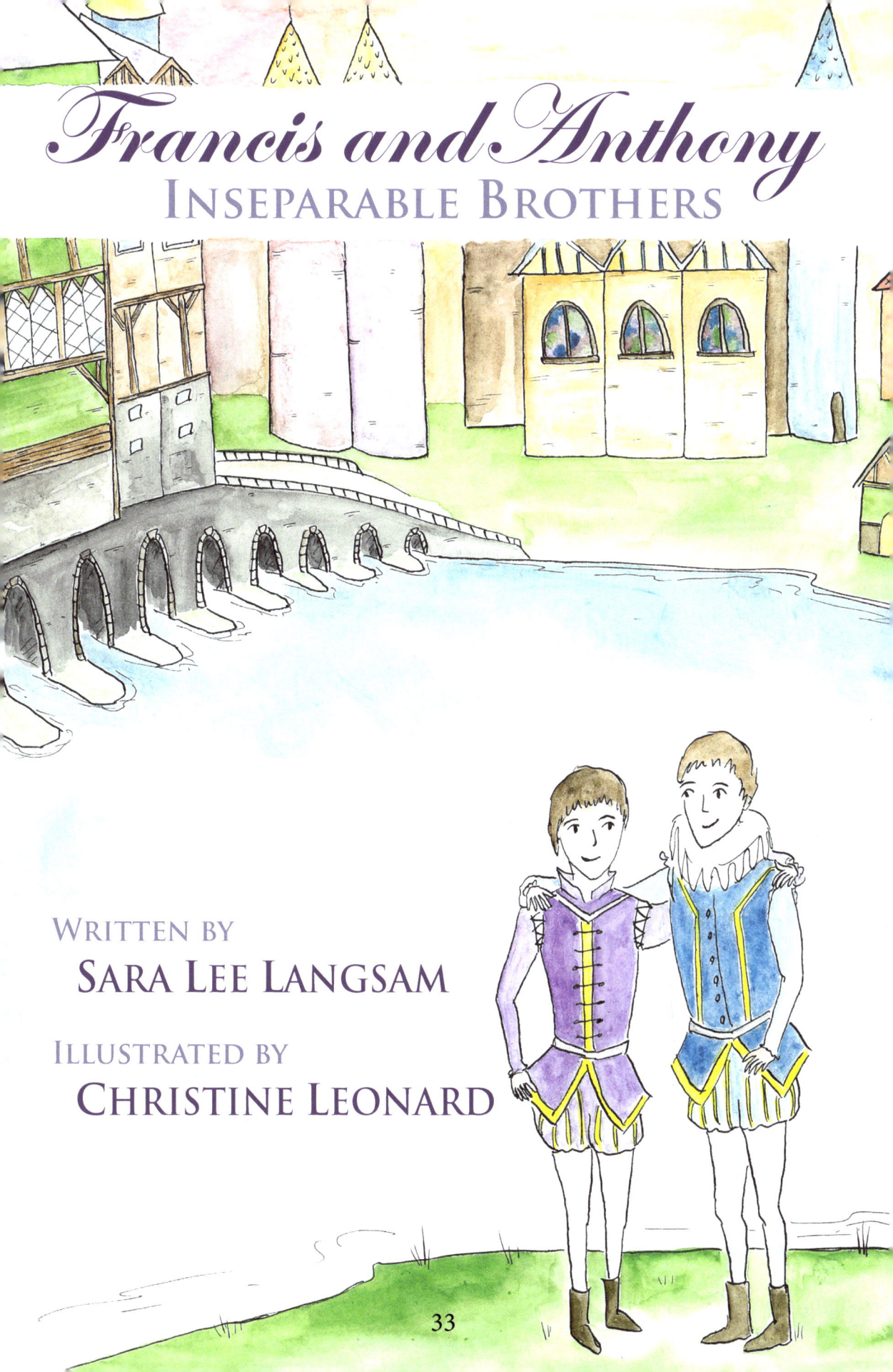

Francis and his older brother Anthony grew up in a loving household under the watchful eyes of their parents.

They thrived in the warmth of a caring environment where learning was very important.

Lady Ann Bacon was very well-educated and had a wonderful collection of books. She spent a lot of time teaching her two boys to read and write.

Sir Nicholas Bacon also had an impressive library of books in English and other languages.

In order to read these books, Francis had to learn many foreign languages.

To make certain that his two boys learned as much as possible, Sir Nicholas brought many tutors into his home to teach his sons. The boys received the finest education in all of England.

This love for learning and for doing one's best was to be the guiding standard for Francis Bacon throughout his life.

When their studying was over, the Bacon brothers would go down to the bank of the Thames. The Thames is a large river that flowed past their house called York House.

As they stood by the river's edge, they watched many activities going on with great interest.

Fishermen were spreading their nets. Barges, special boats with large, long, flat bottoms used for transporting freight, were moving slowly downstream toward London Bridge.

Many smaller boats were carrying people from one bank of the river to the other. They were ferrying them.

Today we call these boats ferries. They are much larger and can carry many more people. We find ferries in many parts of the world.

Is there a ferry near where you live?

When the brothers were not busy watching the activity on the Thames, they would travel by coach with their father to Gorhambury.

Sir Nicholas was building a stone mansion there on a beautiful country estate outside of St. Albans. St. Albans is located 19 miles north of central London and their city residence at York House.

The boys loved to watch the workers building their new home. There were bricklayers, carpenters, and more. The workmen came with ladders and barrows to help them in their work.

A barrow is a flat, rectangular frame with handles at both ends. Two people are needed to carry a barrow from oneplace to another.

Today we recognize the word wheelbarrow as a barrow with wheels. It can be easily moved from one place to another by only one person.

The workmen were good-natured. They were cheerful and friendly. They let the boys climb up and down the building materials. The boys' hands got dirty, and their stockings got torn.

They were having a wonderful time.

The new mansion took five years to complete. It was spacious and beautiful and was surrounded by wide lawns and lovely gardens.

The Bacon brothers spent many happy years there.

When Francis was twelve years old and Anthony fourteen, it was decided that the boys had learned all that they could from Sir Nicholas, Lady Ann, and the tutors.

Francis and Anthony were ready to go to college.

A new adventure lay just over the horizon. Francis and Anthony were sent to Trinity College, part of Cambridge University. They were happy to be together and looked forward to making new friends and learning many new and exciting things.

Biographies

Sara Lee Langsam taught high school Spanish and English as a Second Language in high school and elementary school. Words have always fascinated her and the beauty and meaning of life that can be captured in poetry.

She has a special interest in the life and works of Sir Francis Bacon and a deep desire to make him known to the children of the world. She has also written four books of poetry: *Angels and Fairies and Bright Rainbows,* (original edition), *Angels and Fairies and Bright Rainbows* (expanded edition), *The Voice of the Heart,* and *The Homeward Path,* which includes both poems and essays.

Sara Lee's poems, essays, and children's stories portray on a subtle level the ideas and concepts she has learned in her lifetime of studying the world's many spiritual and religious traditions. The knowledge of these traditions and their role in our everyday life has given the author the opportunity through her books to share with others these vital life-enhancing concepts.

Christine Leonard is a Chinese American science writer and editor living in Philadelphia. As a former freelance illustrator, she worked on young adult novels and children's books.

www.ingramcontent.com/pod-product-compliance
Lightning Source LLC
LaVergne TN
LVHW072113070426
835510LV00002B/28